HOW TO GET OUT OF THE DEBT TRAP

Proven and Effective Formula for Freeing Yourself from Debt

Jason D. Page

Table of Content

About the Author

Jason D. Page is a seasoned financial consultant and educator with over two decades of experience in personal finance. He specializes in helping individuals and families achieve financial stability and independence. Jason graduated with a degree in Economics from the University of Chicago and has worked with various financial institutions, gaining expertise in debt management, investment strategies, and financial planning.

Known for his ability to simplify complex financial concepts, Jason has become a sought-after speaker and workshop leader. His practical advice and approachable style have helped countless individuals develop sound financial habits and achieve their goals. He has also written extensively for prominent financial publications, sharing insights on budgeting, saving, credit management, and retirement planning.

"How to Get Out of the Debt Trap: Proven and Effective Formulas for Freeing Yourself from Debt" reflects Jason's commitment to empowering others. The book offers real-life success stories, practical tools, and step-by-step guidance for escaping debt. In his free time, Jason enjoys hiking with his family and volunteering with organizations that promote financial education. His mission is to provide everyone with the knowledge and tools to achieve financial independence.

Introduction

Debt is a reality for many people. It can be overwhelming and stressful, often feeling like a never ending cycle. Understanding the debt trap is the first step to breaking free from it.

The debt trap is a situation where you owe more money than you can repay. It starts small—maybe with a credit card or a personal loan. Over time, it grows as interest adds up and new debts pile on. Before you know it, you're juggling multiple payments and struggling to keep up.

How does this happen? Life is full of unexpected expenses. Car repairs, medical bills, or even daily living costs can add up quickly. When you don't have enough savings, borrowing seems like the only option. Credit cards and loans provide a quick fix, but they come with high interest rates and fees. This is where the trouble begins.

The psychology of debt plays a big role in this trap. It's easy to think, "I'll pay it off later," or "I need this now." But these thoughts can lead to more borrowing and deeper debt. It's a cycle: borrowing to pay off borrowing. This can feel like being stuck in quicksand—the more you struggle, the deeper you sink.

Assessing your financial situation is crucial. Many people don't realize how much they owe. They avoid looking at their statements or calculating the total debt. This avoidance is understandable—debt can be scary. But facing it head-on is the only way to start the journey to freedom.

Creating a debt repayment plan is the next step. This plan will help you see the path to becoming debt-free. It involves listing all your debts, prioritizing them, and setting up a payment schedule. It might seem daunting, but breaking it down into manageable steps makes it achievable.

Budgeting is another key aspect. Managing your money wisely is essential to avoid falling back into debt. A budget helps you track your income and expenses, ensuring you live within your means. It also highlights areas where you can cut back and save more.

Reducing expenses might mean making some sacrifices. It could be as simple as cooking at home more often or canceling unused subscriptions. Every little bit helps when you're working towards a debt-free life.

Increasing your income is another powerful tool. This doesn't always mean finding a new job. It could involve taking on extra work, freelancing, or even selling items you no longer need. More income means more money to put towards your debt.

Having an emergency fund is crucial. This is a savings cushion that helps cover unexpected costs without resorting to credit. It provides peace of mind and financial stability, preventing future debt.

Prioritizing debt repayment means paying off high-interest debts first. This strategy saves money in the long run and helps reduce the total amount owed faster. It's important to stay consistent and committed to this process.

Managing your credit score is also important. A good credit score can lower interest rates and make borrowing cheaper. Understanding how your score is calculated and taking steps to improve it can benefit your financial health.

Dealing with creditors and debt collectors can be stressful. Knowing your rights and how to communicate effectively can make a big difference. Sometimes, negotiating can lead to reduced payments or better terms.

Debt consolidation is another option to consider. This involves combining all your debts into one loan with a lower interest rate. It simplifies payments and can save money, but it's not without risks.

Bankruptcy should be a last resort. It can provide relief from debt but has long-term consequences on your credit. It's important to understand all options before considering this path.

Building healthy financial habits is essential to staying out of debt. This means being mindful of spending, saving regularly, and avoiding unnecessary borrowing. It's a lifelong commitment to financial well-being.

Avoiding future debt traps requires awareness and planning. Life will always have unexpected costs, but with the right habits and plans in place, you can handle them without falling into debt.

There are many tools and resources available to help with debt management. From apps to financial advisors, seeking help can provide guidance and support.

Real-life success stories can be inspiring. They show that becoming debt-free is possible and provide motivation to keep going.

Staying debt-free is the ultimate goal. It requires ongoing effort and vigilance, but the rewards are worth it. Financial freedom brings peace of mind, security, and the ability to enjoy life without the burden of debt.

In this book, we'll explore all these topics in detail. You'll learn practical strategies and gain the knowledge needed to break free from the debt trap. It's a journey, but one that leads to a brighter, more secure future. Let's take the first step together.

Chapter 1: The Psychology of Debt

Debt isn't just about numbers on a page or bills in the mail. It's about how we think and feel about money. Understanding the psychology of debt can help us break free from its hold.

Why do people go into debt? Sometimes, it's due to an emergency or a big purchase like a car or a house. But often, it's because of everyday spending. It's easy to swipe a credit card for things we want but don't need. Over time, these small purchases add up, and before we know it, we're deep in debt.

Our emotions play a big role in how we handle money. When we're happy, we might celebrate by spending. When we're sad or stressed, shopping can make us feel better, at least for a little while. This is called emotional spending. It's like using money to fill a hole in our hearts. But this quick fix can lead to more problems down the road.

Society also influences our spending habits. We see friends and family with new clothes, gadgets, or vacations, and we want the same. Advertising tells us that buying things will make us happier, more successful, or more attractive. Social media shows us a constant stream of people living their best lives. It's easy to feel left out and think that spending will help us keep up.

There's also the concept of instant gratification. We want things now, not later. Credit cards and loans make it easy to get what we want right away, without having to save up. This can lead to a cycle of borrowing and paying interest, which makes it harder to get out of debt.

Another factor is the way we think about our future selves. It's easy to believe that we'll have more money later to pay off what we borrow now. We tell ourselves, "I'll make more money next year," or "I'll get a bonus and pay this off." But often, that extra money doesn't come, and we're stuck with the debt.

Many people avoid thinking about their debt. They don't open bills or check their balances. This avoidance can make the problem worse. Not knowing how much we owe can create anxiety and make us feel out of control. But facing the debt head-on is the first step to taking control of our finances.

There's also a sense of shame and guilt that comes with debt. People often feel embarrassed about their financial situation. They think they should have done better and made smarter choices. This shame can prevent them from seeking help or talking about their problems, making it harder to find a solution.

It's important to remember that debt is not a moral failing. Many people struggle with debt due to circumstances beyond their control, like job loss, medical bills, or family emergencies. It's a common problem, and there are ways to manage and overcome it.

Understanding the psychology of debt can help us change our habits and attitudes towards money. One effective strategy is to become more mindful about spending. This means thinking carefully about each purchase and asking ourselves if it's necessary. It also means being aware of our emotional triggers and finding healthier ways to cope with stress or sadness.

Setting financial goals can also be motivating. When we have a clear picture of what we want to achieve, like paying off a credit card or saving for a vacation, it's easier to stay focused. Breaking big goals into smaller, manageable steps can make them seem less overwhelming.

Building a support system is another key step. Talking to friends or family about our financial struggles can provide comfort and advice. There are also financial counselors and support groups that can offer guidance and help us stay on track.

Changing our relationship with money takes time and effort. It involves understanding our past behaviors and making a conscious decision to act differently in the future. It's about creating new habits and sticking with them, even when it's challenging.

In this book, we'll explore more about the psychology of debt and how it affects our lives. We'll look at practical ways to change our thinking and behavior, so we can take control of our finances and work towards a debt-free future. By understanding why we do what we do, we can make better choices and build a healthier, happier relationship with money.

Chapter 2: Assessing Your Financial Situation

Before you can get out of debt, you need to know exactly where you stand financially. Assessing your financial situation is like taking a snapshot of your money life. It helps you see the big picture and understand what you need to do next.

First, gather all your financial documents. This includes bank statements, credit card bills, loan statements, and any other records of money you owe or money you have. It might feel overwhelming to see it all in one place, but this step is crucial. You can't fix what you don't know.

Start by listing all your debts. Write down each debt's total amount, the interest rate, and the minimum monthly payment. This might include credit card balances, personal loans, car loans, student loans, and mortgages. Seeing these numbers can be shocking, but remember, you're taking the first step towards taking control.

Next, look at your income. How much money do you bring in each month? Include your salary, any side income, and other sources of money, like child support or government benefits. It's important to have a clear understanding of your total income so you know how much you have to work with.

Now, compare your income to your expenses. Make a list of all your monthly expenses. This includes fixed expenses, like rent or mortgage payments, utilities, insurance, and car payments. Don't forget variable expenses, such as groceries, gas, entertainment, and eating out. Be honest with yourself about what you spend.

If your expenses are higher than your income, you're living beyond your means. This is a common issue that leads to debt. The goal is to either increase your income, reduce your expenses, or both. We'll talk more about these strategies later in the book.

Once you have a clear picture of your income and expenses, it's time to look at your assets and liabilities. Assets are things you own that have value, like your house, car, savings accounts, and investments. Liabilities are what you owe, like your debts. Subtract your liabilities from your assets to find your net worth. This number tells you if you're financially positive or negative.

Having a low or negative net worth can be discouraging, but it's important information. It shows you where you are and gives you a starting point for improvement. Remember, the goal is to increase your assets and decrease your liabilities over time.

Another important part of assessing your financial situation is understanding your credit score. Your credit score is a number that shows how well you manage debt. Lenders use it to decide if they will lend you money and at what interest rate. Check your credit score and get a copy of your credit report. Look for any errors and work on fixing them. A higher credit score can save you money on interest rates.

Emergency savings are also crucial. Do you have money set aside for unexpected expenses? If not, start building an emergency fund. Even a small amount each month can add up over time. An emergency fund provides a safety net, so you don't have to rely on credit when something unexpected happens.

Debt can feel isolating, but you're not alone. Many people face similar challenges, and there are resources to help. Consider talking to a financial advisor or credit counselor. They can provide personalized advice and support.

Creating a budget is a powerful tool for managing your money. A budget helps you track your income and expenses, ensuring you live within your means. Start by listing your monthly income, then your fixed and variable expenses. Allocate a portion of your income to each category, including savings and debt repayment. Stick to your budget as closely as possible, but be flexible. Adjust it as needed to reflect changes in your financial situation.

It's also helpful to set financial goals. What do you want to achieve? This could be paying off a credit card, saving for a vacation, or building an emergency fund. Setting specific, measurable goals gives you something to work towards and helps you stay motivated.

One strategy for paying off debt is the snowball method. Start by paying off your smallest debt first, while making minimum payments on the others. Once the smallest debt is paid off, move to the next smallest, and so on. This method provides quick wins and builds momentum.

Another strategy is the avalanche method. Focus on paying off the debt with the highest interest rate first, while making minimum payments on the others. This saves money on interest in the long run.

Tracking your progress is important. Regularly review your financial situation and celebrate your successes, no matter how small. Seeing your progress can boost your motivation and keep you on track.

Assessing your financial situation is the foundation of getting out of debt. It gives you a clear understanding of where you are and what steps you need to take. It might seem daunting, but taking control of your finances is empowering. With a clear plan and the right tools, you can break free from debt and achieve financial freedom. In this book, we'll explore these strategies in more detail, providing you with the knowledge and confidence to take charge of your financial future.

Chapter 3: Creating a Debt Repayment Plan

Once you understand your financial situation, the next step is to create a debt repayment plan. This plan will be your roadmap to becoming debt-free. It might seem like a big task, but breaking it down into simple steps can make it manageable and even motivating.

First, list all your debts. Write down the name of each creditor, the total amount owed, the interest rate, and the minimum monthly payment. Seeing everything in one place helps you understand what you're up against and makes it easier to plan your repayment strategy.

Next, decide on a repayment strategy. Two popular methods are the snowball method and the avalanche method.

The snowball method involves paying off your smallest debt first, regardless of the interest rate. You continue making minimum payments on all your other debts. Once the smallest debt is paid off, you take the money you were putting toward it and apply it to the next smallest debt. This method gives you quick wins and can be very motivating. Each time you pay off a debt, you feel a sense of accomplishment, which keeps you going.

The avalanche method focuses on paying off the debt with the highest interest rate first. Again, you make minimum payments on all your other debts. Once the highest-interest debt is paid off, you move to the next highest-interest debt. This method saves you money on interest in the long run. It might take longer to see results, but you'll pay less overall.

Choose the method that works best for you. If you need quick wins to stay motivated, the snowball method might be better. If you're more focused on saving money, the avalanche method could be the way to go.

Now, create a budget. Your budget should include all your income and expenses. Allocate a portion of your income to cover your living expenses, like rent, utilities, groceries, and transportation. Then, allocate money to your debt repayment plan. Be sure to include some money for savings and emergencies, too. Sticking to a budget can be challenging, but it's essential for staying on track with your debt repayment plan.

To help stick to your budget, look for ways to cut expenses. This might mean making some sacrifices, like eating out less or canceling subscriptions you don't use. Even small changes can add up over time. Remember, these sacrifices are temporary. Once you're out of debt, you'll have more financial freedom.

Increasing your income can also help speed up your debt repayment. Consider taking on a part-time job, freelancing, or selling items you no longer need. Use this extra money to pay down your debt faster. Every little bit helps.

Set clear, achievable goals for your debt repayment. For example, you might set a goal to pay off a specific debt within six months. Break this goal down into smaller, monthly targets. Achieving these smaller goals will give you a sense of progress and keep you motivated.

It's important to stay organized. Keep track of your payments and your progress. You can use a spreadsheet, a notebook, or an app to monitor your debt repayment. Seeing the balances go down will encourage you to keep going.

Consider setting up automatic payments for your debts. This ensures you never miss a payment and helps you stay consistent. It also takes some of the stress out of managing multiple payments each month.

If you find yourself struggling to make progress, don't hesitate to seek help. A credit counselor can provide advice and support. They can help you create a more detailed plan and offer strategies for managing your money. Sometimes, just talking to someone who understands can make a big difference.

Another helpful step is to communicate with your creditors. If you're having trouble making payments, contact them and explain your situation. Many creditors are willing to work with you to find a solution. They might offer lower interest rates, reduced payments, or a different repayment schedule. It's worth asking for help rather than falling behind on payments.

Avoid taking on new debt while you're working on your repayment plan. It's tempting to use credit for emergencies or big purchases, but this can slow your progress. Focus on paying off what you owe first.

Celebrate your milestones along the way. Paying off debt is a significant achievement, and it's important to acknowledge your hard work. Treat yourself to something small when you reach a goal, but make sure it fits within your budget.

Creating a debt repayment plan is a powerful step toward financial freedom. It gives you a clear path to follow and helps you stay focused on your goal. It might be challenging at times, but with determination and persistence, you can succeed. Remember, the journey to becoming debt-free is a marathon, not a sprint. Each step you take brings you closer to a brighter financial future. In this book, we'll provide more tips and strategies to help you along the way. You can do this!

Chapter 4: Budgeting Basics: Managing Your Money

Budgeting is a key part of managing your money and getting out of debt. It helps you understand where your money goes and ensures you live within your means. Creating a budget might sound boring or difficult, but it can actually be empowering and give you control over your finances.

To start, gather all your financial information. This includes your income, bills, receipts, and bank statements. You need a clear picture of your money coming in and going out. Once you have everything, you're ready to create your budget.

First, list all your sources of income. This could be your salary, freelance work, child support, or any other money you receive regularly. Write down the total amount you earn each month.

Next, make a list of your expenses. Start with your fixed expenses. These are things you have to pay each month, like rent or mortgage, utilities, car payments, insurance, and loan payments. These costs usually stay the same from month to month.

Then, list your variable expenses. These are things that can change each month, like groceries, gas, entertainment, and dining out. Be honest about what you spend. It's easy to underestimate, but knowing the real numbers is important for creating a realistic budget.

After you've listed all your expenses, compare them to your income. Subtract your total expenses from your total income. If you have money left over, you're in good shape. If you're spending more than you earn, it's time to make some changes.

One of the first things to do is look for ways to reduce your variable expenses. This might mean cutting back on eating out, canceling subscriptions you don't use, or finding cheaper alternatives for things you buy regularly. Small changes can add up over time and help you save money.

It's also important to set aside money for savings and emergencies. Aim to save a portion of your income each month, even if it's a small amount. An emergency fund can help cover unexpected expenses, like car repairs or medical bills, so you don't have to rely on credit.

Once you've adjusted your expenses and made room for savings, create a plan for your debt repayment. Allocate a specific amount of your income to paying off your debts each month. Stick to this amount and avoid taking on new debt.

To make budgeting easier, consider using the 50/30/20 rule. This rule suggests that you spend 50% of your income on needs, 30% on wants, and 20% on savings and debt repayment. Needs include things like housing, utilities, groceries, and transportation. Wants are things you enjoy but don't necessarily need, like dining out, entertainment, and hobbies. This simple guideline can help you balance your spending and ensure you're saving enough.

Another helpful tool is a budgeting app or spreadsheet. These tools can track your income and expenses automatically, making it easier to see where your money is going. Many apps also offer features like bill reminders, goal tracking, and spending alerts.

Budgeting is not a one-time task. It's important to review and adjust your budget regularly. Life changes, and so do your financial needs. Check your budget at least once a month to see if you're on track and make any necessary adjustments. If you get a raise, for example, update your budget to reflect your new income and consider increasing your savings or debt repayment.

It's also helpful to set financial goals. What do you want to achieve with your money? This could be paying off a credit card, saving for a vacation, or building an emergency fund. Having clear goals gives you something to work towards and can keep you motivated.

Remember, budgeting is about balance. It's not about depriving yourself of everything you enjoy, but about making conscious choices with your money. It's okay to spend on things you love, as long as you're also saving and paying off debt.

If you find it hard to stick to your budget, try using cash for variable expenses. Withdraw the amount you've allocated for things like groceries and entertainment, and use only that cash for the month. When the cash is gone, you know you've reached your limit.

Building a support system can also help you stay on track. Talk to friends or family members about your budgeting goals. They can offer advice, encouragement, and accountability. There are also online communities and support groups for people working on their finances.

Budgeting can feel overwhelming at first, but it gets easier with practice. The more you work on your budget, the more comfortable you'll become with managing your money. Over time, you'll start to see the benefits of your efforts, like reduced debt, increased savings, and less financial stress.

Chapter 5: Strategies for Reducing Expenses

Reducing expenses is a crucial part of managing your money and getting out of debt. When you spend less, you can save more and pay off your debts faster. Here are some simple and effective strategies to help you cut costs and live within your means.

1. Track Your Spending

The first step to reducing expenses is knowing where your money goes. Keep track of every purchase you make for a month. You can use a notebook, a spreadsheet, or a budgeting app. At the end of the month, review your spending. Look for patterns and areas where you can cut back.

2. Make a Grocery List

Grocery shopping can be a major expense. To save money, always make a list before you go to the store. Stick to the list and avoid impulse buys. Plan your meals for the week and buy only what you need. Cooking at home is usually cheaper and healthier than eating out.

3. Cook in Bulk

Cooking larger meals and freezing the leftovers can save you time and money. When you make a big batch of food, you can use the leftovers for lunches or dinners later in the week. This reduces the need for takeout or expensive convenience foods.

4. Shop Sales and Use Coupons

Take advantage of sales and use coupons whenever possible. Many stores offer loyalty programs that provide discounts and special offers. There are also apps and websites that help you find the best deals and coupons for your favorite stores.

5. Cut Down on Dining Out

Eating out can be fun, but it's also expensive. Try to limit how often you dine out. Instead, have friends over for a potluck or cook a special meal at home. When you do go out, look for deals, like happy hour specials or discount days.

6. Cancel Unused Subscriptions

Many people have subscriptions they don't use or need. Review your subscriptions, such as streaming services, magazines, and gym memberships. Cancel any that you don't use regularly. This can free up a surprising amount of money each month.

7. Review Your Bills

Take a close look at your monthly bills. Are you paying for services you don't need? For example, you might have a cable package with channels you never watch. Consider switching to a cheaper plan or cutting cable altogether and using a streaming service.

8. Save on Utilities

Small changes can lead to big savings on your utility bills. Turn off lights when you leave a room, unplug electronics when they're not in use, and lower the thermostat a few degrees in the winter. Using energy-efficient appliances and light bulbs can also reduce your bills.

9. Use Public Transportation

If you live in an area with good public transportation, consider using it instead of driving. This can save you money on gas, parking, and car maintenance. If public transportation isn't an option, try carpooling with coworkers or friends to share the cost.

10. Buy Second Hand

Before buying something new, check out secondhand options. Thrift stores, consignment shops, and online marketplaces often have gently used items at a fraction of the cost. This is especially great for clothes, furniture, and household items.

11. Limit Your Entertainment Spending

Entertainment is important, but it doesn't have to be expensive. Look for free or low-cost activities in your area, like community events, parks, and libraries. Many places offer free days or discounts, such as museums or theaters. Hosting a game night or movie night at home can also be a fun and affordable way to spend time with friends.

12. Plan Your Purchases

Before making a big purchase, take some time to think about it. Do you really need it? Can you afford it? Sometimes waiting a few days can help you decide if it's worth the money. If you still want it, look for the best price and consider buying during sales events.

13. Use Cash for Discretionary Spending

Using cash instead of credit or debit cards can help you stick to your budget. Withdraw a set amount of cash for discretionary spending, like dining out or entertainment, and use only that money. When the cash is gone, you know you've reached your limit.

14. DIY When You Can

Doing things yourself can save a lot of money. Learn to do basic home repairs, cook meals from scratch, and take care of your lawn or garden. There are plenty of tutorials online to help you get started. Plus, DIY projects can be rewarding and fun.

15. Negotiate Bills and Fees

Don't be afraid to negotiate your bills and fees. Call your service providers and ask for discounts or better rates. This can include your cable, internet, phone, and insurance bills. Many companies are willing to offer lower rates to keep your business.

16. Set Savings Goals

Setting specific savings goals can motivate you to reduce expenses. Whether it's saving for a vacation, a new car, or an emergency fund, having a clear goal helps you stay focused. Track your progress and celebrate when you reach your milestones.

17. Avoid Impulse Purchases

Impulse purchases can add up quickly and derail your budget. Before buying something on a whim, give yourself some time to think about it. Ask yourself if you really need it and if it fits within your budget. Waiting even 24 hours can help you make more thoughtful decisions.

18. Find Free or Low-Cost Hobbies

Hobbies are important, but they don't have to be expensive. Look for free or low-cost activities you enjoy, like hiking, reading, or crafting. Many communities offer free classes and events, so check out local resources for fun and affordable ways to spend your time.

19. Review Your Insurance Policies

Make sure you're not overpaying for insurance. Review your policies and shop around for better rates. Sometimes bundling your home and auto insurance can save you money. Also, consider raising your deductibles to lower your premiums, but make sure you have enough savings to cover the higher deductible if needed.

20. Make Use of Loyalty Programs

Many stores and restaurants offer loyalty programs that provide discounts, coupons, and rewards. Sign up for these programs and use them regularly. Over time, the savings can add up.

21. Embrace Minimalism

Adopting a minimalist lifestyle can help you focus on what's truly important and reduce unnecessary spending. This doesn't mean you have to get rid of everything, but it encourages you to be more intentional with your purchases and appreciate what you already have.

22. Plan for Big Expenses

If you know you have a big expense coming up, like a car repair or holiday shopping, plan for it in advance. Set aside money each month to cover these costs. This way, you won't have to rely on credit or dip into your savings when the time comes.

23. Avoid Bank Fees

Bank fees can add up quickly. Look for a bank account with no monthly fees and avoid overdrafts by keeping track of your balance. Many banks offer alerts to help you stay on top of your account and avoid unnecessary charges.

24. Consider Downsizing

If your housing costs are a big part of your budget, consider downsizing. Moving to a smaller home or a more affordable area can significantly reduce your expenses. This might not be an option for everyone, but it's worth considering if you're struggling to make ends meet.

25. Make Saving Fun

Find ways to make saving money enjoyable. Challenge yourself to a no-spend day or week, where you don't spend any money except on essentials. Turn it into a game with your family or friends and see who can save the most. Small, fun challenges can help you stay motivated.

Reducing expenses takes effort and discipline, but the rewards are worth it. By cutting back on unnecessary spending, you can free up more money to save and pay off debt. Remember, every little bit helps. Even small changes can make a big difference over time. In this book, we'll explore more strategies and tips to help you manage your money and achieve financial freedom. You have the power to take control of your finances and create a secure, debt-free future.

Chapter 6: Increasing Your Income: Practical Tips

Getting out of debt and achieving financial freedom often requires more than just cutting expenses. Increasing your income can significantly speed up your debt repayment and help you build savings. Here are some practical and straightforward ways to boost your earnings.

1. Ask for a Raise

If you have been in your job for a while and have been performing well, it might be time to ask for a raise. Do some research to find out what others in your position are earning. Prepare a list of your accomplishments and contributions to the company. Schedule a meeting with your boss and confidently present your case. Even if you don't get a raise immediately, it shows your employer that you value your work and are looking to grow.

2. Look for a Better-Paying Job

Sometimes, the best way to increase your income is to find a new job that pays more. Update your resume and start looking for job openings in your field. Network with people in your industry and let them know you are looking for new opportunities. Be open to roles that might offer better pay and benefits, even if they are a bit different from your current job.

3. Take on a Part-Time Job

A part-time job can provide extra income to help pay down debt or build savings. Look for opportunities that fit your schedule, such as evenings or weekends. Retail, food service, and gig economy jobs like driving for a rideshare service or delivering food can be good options. While it might mean working more hours, the extra money can make a big difference.

4. Freelance or Consult

If you have skills that are in demand, consider freelancing or consulting. Many companies and individuals need help with writing, graphic design, programming, marketing, and other tasks. Websites like Upwork, Fiverr, and Freelancer can connect you with clients. Freelancing allows you to work on your own schedule and take on as much work as you can handle.

5. Start a Side Business

Starting a small business can be a great way to increase your income. Think about what you enjoy and what skills you have. You could start a home-based business, such as baking, pet sitting, tutoring, or crafting. Use social media and local community boards to advertise your services. Starting small can help you manage risks and grow your business gradually.

6. Rent Out a Room or Property

If you have extra space in your home, consider renting it out for extra income. Websites like Airbnb make it easy to list a room or property for short-term rentals. If you have a second property or a vacation home, renting it out can also provide a steady stream of income. Just make sure to check local regulations and requirements.

7. Sell Unwanted Items

Look around your home for items you no longer need or use. Selling these items can bring in some extra cash. Use online marketplaces like eBay, Craigslist, or Facebook Marketplace to list your items. You can also have a garage sale or visit a consignment shop. Decluttering your home can also make it feel more organized and peaceful.

8. Offer Services in Your Community

Think about services you can offer to people in your community. This could include lawn care, house cleaning, babysitting, dog walking, or handyman services. Create flyers or business cards to advertise your services. Word of mouth can also be a powerful tool, so let your friends and neighbors know you are available.

9. Participate in Paid Surveys and Studies

There are companies that pay for your opinions. Sign up for paid survey websites and participate in studies. While this won't make you rich, it can provide some extra income for minimal effort. Just be sure to use reputable sites and avoid scams.

10. Teach or Tutor

If you have expertise in a particular subject, consider teaching or tutoring. You can offer your services to students who need help with their schoolwork or to adults looking to learn new skills.

Tutoring can be done in person or online. Websites like Tutor.com and Wyzant can connect you with students.

11. Take Advantage of Cashback and Rewards Programs

Many credit cards and shopping apps offer cashback and rewards for your purchases. Make sure you're taking advantage of these programs to earn money back on things you already buy. Just be careful not to overspend just to earn rewards.

12. Invest in Your Education and Skills

Sometimes, increasing your income means investing in yourself. Consider taking courses or earning certifications that can help you qualify for higher-paying jobs. Many community colleges and online platforms offer affordable classes. Improving your skills can make you more valuable to employers and open up new opportunities.

13. Write a Book or Create Online Content

If you enjoy writing or creating content, consider writing a book or starting a blog, YouTube channel, or podcast. While it takes time to build an audience, it can eventually lead to income through ads, sponsorships, or sales. Sharing your knowledge and passions can also be a rewarding experience.

14. Participate in the Gig Economy

The gig economy offers various ways to earn extra income on a flexible schedule. This includes driving for rideshare services, delivering groceries or food, and completing tasks for people through platforms like TaskRabbit. These gigs can be a good way to earn money on your own terms.

15. Sell Handmade or Customized Products

If you are crafty or have a talent for making things, consider selling handmade or customized products. Platforms like Etsy allow you to reach a wide audience. Whether it's jewelry, clothing, artwork, or home decor, turning your hobby into a business can provide extra income.

16. Offer Virtual Assistance

Many businesses and entrepreneurs need help with administrative tasks. Offering virtual assistant services can be a flexible way to earn extra money. This can include tasks like managing emails, scheduling appointments, and social media management.

17. Provide Caregiving Services

If you enjoy helping others, consider offering caregiving services. This could include childcare, eldercare, or pet sitting. Caregivers are in high demand, and these services can be both rewarding and lucrative.

18. Work Seasonal Jobs

Seasonal jobs can provide a temporary boost to your income. Retail stores often hire extra help during the holiday season, and there are opportunities for work during the summer months, such as lifeguarding or working at a camp.

19. Rent Out Your Car

If you don't use your car all the time, consider renting it out through services like Turo. This can help you earn money from a valuable asset that might otherwise sit unused.

20. Network and Market Yourself

Don't underestimate the power of networking. Let people know you're looking for ways to increase your income. Attend industry events, join professional groups, and use social media to connect with potential clients or employers. Marketing yourself effectively can open up new opportunities.

Chapter 7: The Importance of an Emergency Fund

An emergency fund is like a financial safety net. It's money set aside to help you cover unexpected expenses or financial emergencies without going into debt. Having an emergency fund is crucial because life is full of surprises, and being prepared can give you peace of mind and financial security.

1. Protection Against Unexpected Expenses

Life can be unpredictable. Your car might break down, your pet might get sick, or you might face a sudden job loss. These unexpected expenses can put a strain on your finances if you're not prepared. An emergency fund allows you to cover these costs without having to rely on credit cards or loans, which can lead to debt and financial stress.

2. Peace of Mind

Knowing you have money set aside for emergencies can reduce anxiety and stress. You'll feel more confident knowing that you can handle unexpected financial setbacks without disrupting your daily life or long-term financial goals. This sense of security can improve your overall well-being and mental health.

3. Avoiding Debt

Using credit cards or loans to cover emergency expenses can lead to high-interest charges and debt that can be difficult to pay off. An emergency fund allows you to pay for unexpected costs upfront, avoiding interest payments and the cycle of debt. It helps you maintain financial independence and stability.

4. Flexibility and Freedom

Having an emergency fund gives you flexibility in your financial decisions. You can take advantage of opportunities or make important decisions without worrying about immediate financial consequences. Whether it's pursuing a new job, moving to a new city, or investing in your education, having savings gives you the freedom to take calculated risks.

5. Smoother Budgeting

An emergency fund can help you stick to your budget and financial plan. It acts as a buffer against unexpected expenses that can derail your financial goals. Instead of scrambling to find money or cutting back on essentials, you can use your emergency fund to stay on track and continue working towards your priorities.

6. Faster Recovery from Financial Setbacks

Financial setbacks, such as medical emergencies or unexpected home repairs, can happen to anyone. Having an emergency fund allows you to recover more quickly and get back on your feet. It reduces the impact of these setbacks on your overall financial stability and helps you bounce back stronger.

7. Financial Independence

Building an emergency fund is a step towards financial independence. It means you are less reliant on others or external sources of funding during tough times. You can rely on yourself and your savings to weather financial storms and achieve your long-term financial goals.

8. Building Financial Discipline

Creating and maintaining an emergency fund requires discipline and commitment. It encourages responsible financial habits, such as saving regularly and prioritizing financial security. Over time, these habits can lead to improved financial health and resilience.

9. Protecting Your Investments

If you have investments or retirement savings, an emergency fund can protect them during times of financial hardship. Instead of cashing out investments or tapping into retirement accounts prematurely, you can use your emergency fund to cover immediate expenses while allowing your investments to continue growing.

10. Setting an Example

Having an emergency fund sets a positive example for others, such as family members or children. It demonstrates the importance of financial preparedness and responsible money management. By prioritizing savings, you can inspire others to take control of their finances and build their own safety nets.

An emergency fund is not just a financial cushion; it's a cornerstone of financial stability and peace of mind. It provides protection against unexpected expenses, helps you avoid debt, and gives you the freedom to make decisions without financial stress. Building and maintaining an emergency fund should be a priority for everyone, regardless of income or financial situation. Start small, save regularly, and watch your emergency fund grow. Your future self will thank you for the security and resilience it provides.

Chapter 8: Prioritizing Debt Repayment

Prioritizing debt repayment is essential for achieving financial freedom and reducing financial stress. Whether you have credit card debt, student loans, or other obligations, creating a plan to pay off debt can help you take control of your finances and work towards your goals. Here are some simple yet effective strategies to prioritize debt repayment.

1. Understand Your Debt

The first step in prioritizing debt repayment is to understand exactly what you owe. Make a list of all your debts, including the total amount owed, interest rates, and minimum monthly payments. This will give you a clear picture of your financial obligations and help you prioritize which debts to pay off first.

2. Organize Your Debts

Once you have a list of your debts, organize them based on interest rates and terms. High-interest debts, such as credit card balances, usually cost you more in the long run. Prioritize paying off these debts first to minimize interest charges and reduce your overall debt load faster.

3. Create a Budget

Creating a budget is crucial for effective debt repayment. Track your income and expenses to determine how much money you can allocate towards debt repayment each month. Cut back on discretionary spending and redirect those funds towards paying off your debts. Every dollar counts towards reaching your financial goals.

4. Use the Debt Snowball Method

The debt snowball method is a strategy where you focus on paying off your smallest debt first while making minimum payments on larger debts. Once the smallest debt is paid off, use the money you were paying towards it to tackle the next smallest debt. This method provides motivation by achieving quick wins and building momentum towards larger debts.

5. Consider the Debt Avalanche Method

Alternatively, the debt avalanche method prioritizes paying off debts with the highest interest rates first. By tackling high-interest debts early, you reduce the amount of interest you pay over time and accelerate your debt repayment progress. This method can save you money in interest charges compared to other repayment strategies.

6. Increase Your Income

Finding ways to increase your income can accelerate your debt repayment efforts. Look for opportunities to earn extra money through part-time jobs, freelancing, or selling unwanted items.

Use the additional income to make larger payments towards your debts and achieve your financial goals sooner.

7. Negotiate Lower Interest Rates

Contact your creditors to negotiate lower interest rates on your debts, especially credit cards. A lower interest rate means more of your payment goes towards reducing the principal balance, helping you pay off debt faster. Explain your situation and ask if they can offer you a better rate based on your payment history and creditworthiness.

8. Avoid Taking on New Debt

While repaying existing debt, avoid taking on new debt whenever possible. Cut up credit cards or leave them at home to resist the temptation of impulse purchases. Focus on living within your means and using cash or debit for purchases. This discipline will prevent your debt from increasing and derail your debt repayment plan.

9. Celebrate Milestones

As you make progress towards paying off your debts, celebrate milestones along the way. Whether it's paying off a credit card balance or making your final student loan payment, acknowledge your achievements. Celebrating milestones motivates you to continue working towards your financial goals and reinforces positive financial habits.

10. Seek Support

Managing debt can be challenging, so don't hesitate to seek support from family, friends, or financial professionals. Join online communities or forums where you can share experiences and learn from others who are on a similar journey. Support and encouragement can keep you motivated during difficult times and help you stay focused on your goals.

Prioritizing debt repayment is a proactive step towards financial stability and independence. By understanding your debt, creating a budget, and using effective repayment strategies like the debt snowball or avalanche methods, you can take control of your finances and achieve your goals. Stay disciplined, track your progress, and celebrate your successes along the way. With determination and commitment, you can successfully repay your debts and build a solid foundation for a brighter financial future.

Chapter 9: Understanding and Managing Credit Scores

Your credit score is a three-digit number that represents your creditworthiness. It's a crucial factor that lenders, landlords, and even employers use to assess your financial reliability. Understanding how credit scores work and managing them effectively can open doors to better financial opportunities and save you money in interest rates. Here's what you need to know:

What is a Credit Score?

A credit score is a numerical representation of your credit history. It reflects how likely you are to repay borrowed money on time. Scores typically range from 300 to 850, with higher scores indicating lower credit risk. Factors that influence your credit score include your payment history, amount of debt owed, length of credit history, types of credit accounts, and new credit inquiries.

Why is Your Credit Score Important?

Your credit score impacts many aspects of your financial life:

- Loan Approvals: Lenders use your credit score to determine whether to approve your loan applications and what interest rates to offer you. A higher score can qualify you for lower interest rates and better loan terms.

- Credit Card Applications: Credit card issuers assess your credit score when you apply for a credit card. A good score can lead to higher credit limits and more favorable terms.

- Renting an Apartment: Landlords may check your credit score as part of the rental application process. A higher score can increase your chances of being approved for a lease.

- Insurance Premiums: Some insurance companies use credit scores to determine your premiums for auto, homeowner's, or renter's insurance policies.

- Employment Opportunities: Certain employers may review your credit history as part of the hiring process, particularly for positions involving financial responsibilities.

How Credit Scores Are Calculated

Credit scores are calculated based on information from your credit report, which is maintained by credit bureaus (such as Experian, TransUnion, and Equifax). Key factors include:

- Payment History (35%): Your track record of making on-time payments on credit accounts and loans.

- Credit Utilization (30%): The amount of credit you're currently using compared to your total available credit limits. Keeping this ratio low can positively impact your score.

- Length of Credit History (15%): How long you've been using credit. Longer credit histories generally lead to higher scores, assuming a positive payment history.

- Credit Mix (10%): The variety of credit accounts you have, such as credit cards, installment loans, and mortgages.

- New Credit (10%): Recent inquiries for credit and new account openings. Opening multiple new accounts in a short period can temporarily lower your score.

Tips for Managing Your Credit Score

1. Pay Bills on Time: Consistently paying bills on or before their due dates is the most important factor in maintaining a good credit score.

2. Monitor Your Credit Report: Regularly check your credit report for errors or unauthorized accounts. You can request a free credit report annually from each of the major credit bureaus at AnnualCreditReport.com.

3. Keep Credit Card Balances Low: Aim to use no more than 30% of your available credit limit on each card to maintain a healthy credit utilization ratio.

4. Avoid Closing Old Accounts: Closing older accounts can shorten your credit history and potentially lower your score. Instead, keep them open and use them occasionally to keep them active.

5. Limit New Credit Applications: Apply for new credit only when necessary. Each application can result in a hard inquiry on your credit report, which can temporarily lower your score.

6. Consider Credit Building Tools: If you have a limited credit history or a low score, consider options like secured credit cards or becoming an authorized user on someone else's credit card to build a positive credit history.

Understanding and managing your credit score is essential for financial success. By maintaining good credit habits, monitoring your credit report regularly, and making informed financial decisions, you can improve your creditworthiness over time. A strong credit score opens doors to better interest rates on loans, lower insurance premiums, and greater financial opportunities. Take control of your credit today to secure a brighter financial future tomorrow.

Chapter 10: Dealing with Creditors and Debt Collectors

Dealing with creditors and debt collectors can be intimidating, but understanding your rights and taking proactive steps can help you manage the situation effectively. Whether you're struggling to make payments or disputing a debt, here's how to handle interactions with creditors and debt collectors in a clear and assertive manner.

Understanding Creditors and Debt Collectors

Creditors are entities to whom you owe money, such as banks, credit card companies, or lenders. When you fall behind on payments, creditors may hire debt collectors to recover the debt on their behalf. Debt collectors are third-party agencies or companies that specialize in collecting debts. It's important to distinguish between original creditors and debt collectors when communicating about your debts.

Know Your Rights

Under the Fair Debt Collection Practices Act (FDCPA), you have rights when dealing with debt collectors. These rights include:

- Protection from Harassment: Debt collectors cannot harass, threaten, or use abusive language when communicating with you.

- Verification of Debt: You have the right to request verification of the debt in writing within 30 days of initial contact. Debt collectors must provide information about the debt, such as the amount owed and the original creditor.

- Dispute Debt: If you believe a debt is inaccurate or you don't owe it, you can dispute the debt with the collector. They must cease collection efforts until they provide verification of the debt.

Steps to Deal with Creditors and Debt Collectors

1. Stay Calm and Communicate: When contacted by a creditor or debt collector, stay calm and listen carefully. Avoid ignoring their calls or letters, as this can escalate the situation. Respond promptly to discuss your options.

2. Verify the Debt: If you receive a collection notice, verify the debt by requesting written validation. This ensures that the debt is accurate and provides details about the original creditor and the amount owed.

3. Negotiate a Payment Plan: If you acknowledge the debt but can't afford to pay it in full, negotiate a payment plan with the creditor or debt collector.

Offer to pay what you can realistically afford each month. Get the agreement in writing before making any payments.

4. Understand Statute of Limitations: Debts have a statute of limitations, which varies by state and type of debt. After this period, creditors cannot sue you to collect the debt. Be aware of the statute of limitations before making any payments or negotiations.

5. Document Everything: Keep records of all communications with creditors and debt collectors, including dates, times, names of representatives, and details discussed. This documentation can be helpful if there are disputes or legal issues later on.

6. Seek Financial Counseling: If you're overwhelmed by debt or struggling to negotiate with creditors, consider seeking help from a non-profit credit counseling agency. They can provide

guidance on managing debt, creating a budget, and negotiating with creditors.

7. Know When to Seek Legal Advice: If you believe a creditor or debt collector is violating your rights under the FDCPA or engaging in illegal practices, consult with a consumer rights attorney. They can advise you on your legal options and help protect your rights.

Dealing with creditors and debt collectors requires patience, assertiveness, and knowledge of your rights. By staying informed, communicating clearly, and taking proactive steps, you can effectively manage your debts and work towards financial stability. Remember, you have rights under the law, and you don't have to face debt collection efforts alone. Take control of your finances and advocate for yourself during challenging times.

Chapter 11: The Power of Negotiation: Reducing Your Debt

Negotiation is a powerful tool when it comes to managing and reducing your debt. Whether you're dealing with credit card debt, medical bills, or other financial obligations, learning how to negotiate effectively can help you save money, lower interest rates, and create manageable repayment plans. Here's how to harness the power of negotiation to take control of your finances:

Understanding the Importance of Negotiation
Negotiation allows you to work directly with creditors or debt collectors to find mutually beneficial solutions. It empowers you to advocate for yourself and explore options that can make debt

repayment more affordable and less stressful. By negotiating, you can potentially:

- Reduce Debt Amounts: Creditors may be willing to accept a lower amount than what you owe as a settlement.

- Lower Interest Rates: Negotiating lower interest rates can save you money over time and make monthly payments more manageable.

- Establish Payment Plans: You can negotiate structured payment plans that fit your budget and allow you to repay debts in smaller, more manageable increments.

- Avoid Collection Actions: Negotiating can help prevent aggressive collection actions, such as lawsuits or wage garnishments, by reaching agreements with creditors.

Steps to Effective Negotiation

1. Gather Information: Before negotiating, gather all relevant information about your debts, including current balances, interest rates, and any previous communications with creditors or collectors. Understanding your financial situation will strengthen your negotiating position.

2. Prepare a Budget: Create a detailed budget that outlines your income, expenses, and available funds for debt repayment. Knowing your financial limits and capabilities will help you propose realistic payment options during negotiations.

3. Contact Creditors Early: Don't wait until you're behind on payments or in collections. Contact creditors as soon as you anticipate financial difficulties or foresee challenges in making payments. Early communication shows your willingness to address the issue responsibly.

4. Be Polite and Professional: Approach negotiations with a polite and respectful attitude. Express your willingness to resolve the debt and highlight your commitment to honoring your financial obligations. Building a positive rapport with creditors can lead to more favorable outcomes.

5. Propose a Settlement: If you can afford to make a lump-sum payment, consider proposing a settlement offer to creditors. Offer to pay a percentage of the total debt amount in exchange for having the remainder forgiven. Make sure to get any settlement agreements in writing before making payments.

6. Negotiate Interest Rates: If high interest rates are contributing to your debt burden, negotiate with creditors to lower them. Highlight your repayment history and inquire about any promotional rates or hardship programs that may be available.

7. Explore Hardship Programs: Many creditors offer hardship programs for borrowers facing financial difficulties. These programs may include temporary reductions in interest rates, waived fees, or extended repayment terms. Inquire about eligibility and how to enroll.

8. Seek Professional Help if Needed: If negotiations become complex or overwhelming, consider seeking assistance from a reputable credit counseling agency or financial advisor. These professionals can provide guidance, negotiate on your behalf, and help you navigate challenging financial situations.

Benefits of Successful Negotiation

- Financial Relief: Negotiating reduced debt amounts or lower interest rates can provide immediate financial relief and improve your ability to manage monthly payments.

- Avoiding Bankruptcy: Effective negotiation can help you avoid more drastic measures like bankruptcy, which can have long-term financial consequences.

- Rebuilding Credit: By honoring negotiated agreements and making timely payments, you can begin rebuilding your credit history and improving your credit score over time.

Negotiation is a valuable skill that can significantly impact your financial well-being. By approaching creditors or debt collectors with transparency, respect, and a clear plan, you can achieve favorable outcomes and regain control of your finances. Don't hesitate to explore negotiation strategies and options that align with your financial goals. With determination and persistence, you can reduce your debt burden and pave the way towards a more secure financial future.

Chapter 12: The Pros and Cons of Debt Consolidation

Debt consolidation is a strategy where you combine multiple debts into a single new loan or repayment plan. It's designed to simplify your finances and potentially reduce your overall interest costs. However, like any financial strategy, there are both advantages and disadvantages to consider before deciding if debt consolidation is right for you.

Pros of Debt Consolidation

1. Simplified Repayment: Instead of juggling multiple payments each month, debt consolidation allows you to make one single payment. This can make managing your finances easier and reduce the risk of missing payments.

2. Lower Interest Rates: If you qualify for a consolidation loan with a lower interest rate than your current debts, you could save money on interest payments over time. This can help you pay off your debt faster.

3. Fixed Repayment Terms: Consolidation loans often come with fixed repayment terms, which means you know exactly when your debt will be paid off. This predictability can make budgeting more manageable.

4. Potential for Lower Monthly Payments: By extending the repayment period or securing a lower interest rate, debt consolidation can reduce your monthly payment amount. This can free up cash flow for other financial goals.

5. Improvement in Credit Score: If you use debt consolidation to pay off high-interest credit card

debt, it can lower your credit utilization ratio and improve your credit score over time.

6. Avoiding Default: Debt consolidation can prevent defaulting on loans or credit cards, which can lead to negative consequences such as late fees, penalties, and damage to your credit score.

Cons of Debt Consolidation

1. Additional Costs: Depending on the terms of the consolidation loan, you may incur fees, such as origination fees or balance transfer fees. Be sure to factor these costs into your decision.

2. Risk of Accruing More Debt: Consolidating debts doesn't eliminate them; it simply moves them to a new account. There's a risk of running up new debts on the credit cards or loans that have been paid off through consolidation.

3. Longer Repayment Period: Extending the repayment period to lower monthly payments can mean paying more in total interest over the life of the loan. It's important to compare total costs before consolidating.

4. Credit Score Impact: Applying for a consolidation loan or new credit account can result in a temporary dip in your credit score due to the credit inquiry and the new account opening. However, timely payments on the consolidation loan can mitigate this impact over time.

5. Not Suitable for All Debts: Some types of debt, such as federal student loans, have specific benefits and repayment options that may not be available through consolidation. Evaluate the terms and benefits of each debt carefully.

6. Risk of Losing Assets: If you use a secured loan (backed by collateral like your home or car) for

debt consolidation and cannot repay the loan, you risk losing the asset used as collateral.

Is Debt Consolidation Right for You?

Debt consolidation can be a valuable tool for simplifying payments and reducing interest costs, but it's important to weigh the pros and cons based on your individual financial situation. Consider factors such as your credit score, total debt amount, interest rates, and repayment terms before making a decision. If you're uncertain, consult with a financial advisor or credit counselor who can provide personalized guidance and help you explore all available options.

Debt consolidation offers potential benefits like simplified repayment, lower interest rates, and improved credit scores. However, it also comes with costs and risks that should be carefully considered. By understanding the pros and cons of debt consolidation and assessing your financial goals, you can make an informed decision that supports your journey towards financial stability and debt-free living.

Chapter 13:
Bankruptcy: Last
Resort Options

Bankruptcy is a legal process designed to provide individuals or businesses overwhelmed by debt with a fresh financial start. While it offers relief from overwhelming debt burdens, bankruptcy should be considered a last resort due to its long-term financial consequences and impact on creditworthiness. Here's what you need to know about bankruptcy in simple terms:

Understanding Bankruptcy

Bankruptcy is governed by federal law and involves filing a petition in court. There are different types of bankruptcy, but the most common for individuals are Chapter 7 and Chapter 13:

1. Chapter 7 Bankruptcy: Also known as liquidation bankruptcy, Chapter 7 involves selling off non-exempt assets to pay creditors. Remaining qualifying debts may be discharged (eliminated), providing a fresh start. Not all debts can be discharged, such as child support or student loans.

2. Chapter 13 Bankruptcy: Often called reorganization bankruptcy, Chapter 13 involves creating a repayment plan to pay off debts over three to five years. You can keep your assets, but you must have a regular income to qualify.

Pros of Bankruptcy

1. Debt Relief: Bankruptcy can discharge qualifying debts, relieving you of financial obligations and stopping creditor collection actions.

2. Fresh Start: Bankruptcy provides an opportunity to rebuild your financial life without overwhelming debt.

3. Automatic Stay: Filing for bankruptcy triggers an automatic stay, halting most collection efforts, lawsuits, foreclosures, and wage garnishments.

4. Legal Protection: Bankruptcy offers legal protection from creditors and their collection activities.

Cons of Bankruptcy

1. Credit Impact: Bankruptcy stays on your credit report for up to 10 years, negatively impacting your credit score and ability to obtain credit in the future.

2. Asset Loss: In Chapter 7 bankruptcy, non-exempt assets may be sold to repay creditors.

Chapter 13 requires a repayment plan, which may restrict your disposable income.

3. Costs and Fees: Bankruptcy involves court and attorney fees, which can be substantial depending on the complexity of your case.

4. Public Record: Bankruptcy filings are public records, which may affect your reputation and future employment opportunities.

Is Bankruptcy Right for You?
Bankruptcy should only be considered after exploring all other options, such as debt consolidation, negotiation, or credit counseling. It's generally recommended if:

- You have unmanageable debt that cannot be resolved through other means.
- You face imminent foreclosure or repossession.

- Your income is insufficient to repay debts over a reasonable period.

Alternatives to Bankruptcy

Before filing for bankruptcy, consider alternatives such as:

- Negotiating with creditors for lower interest rates or payment plans.
- Enrolling in a debt management plan through a credit counseling agency.
- Selling assets or tapping into retirement savings (with caution) to repay debts.

Seeking Legal and Financial Advice

Consulting with a bankruptcy attorney or financial advisor can provide personalized guidance based on your specific circumstances. They can explain the legal implications, assess alternatives, and help you navigate the bankruptcy process if it's determined to be the best option.

Bankruptcy is a serious financial decision with long-lasting consequences. While it offers relief from overwhelming debt, it should be considered only as a last resort after exploring all other options. Understanding the pros and cons of bankruptcy and seeking professional advice can help you make an informed decision that supports your long-term financial well-being.

Chapter 14: Building Healthy Financial Habits

Building healthy financial habits is key to achieving financial stability and securing your future. Whether you're just starting your financial journey or looking to improve your current habits, adopting these practices can help you manage money effectively and work towards your financial goals.

1. Create a Budget

A budget is a foundational tool for managing your finances. Start by listing your income and expenses to understand where your money is going each month. Allocate funds for necessities like rent, utilities, groceries, and transportation, and set aside savings for emergencies and future goals. Track your spending to ensure you stay within your budget and adjust as needed.

2. Save Regularly

Saving money regularly, no matter how small the amount, is crucial for building financial security. Aim to save a portion of your income each month, even if it's just a small percentage. Set up automatic transfers to a savings account to make saving effortless. Over time, your savings will grow, providing a safety net for unexpected expenses and helping you achieve long-term goals like buying a home or retiring comfortably.

3. Pay Bills on Time

Paying bills on time is essential for maintaining good credit and avoiding late fees and penalties. Set up reminders or automatic payments to ensure bills are paid by their due dates. If you're struggling to make payments, contact creditors or service providers to discuss payment plans or alternative arrangements.

4. Manage Debt Wisely

If you have debt, develop a strategy to manage it effectively. Pay more than the minimum payment whenever possible to reduce interest charges and pay off debt faster. Prioritize high-interest debts first while making at least minimum payments on other debts. Avoid taking on new debt unless absolutely necessary, and consider consolidating high-interest debts if it helps lower overall costs.

5. Build and Maintain Good Credit

Your credit history and credit score impact your ability to borrow money and obtain favorable interest rates. Pay bills on time, keep credit card balances low relative to credit limits, and avoid opening multiple new accounts in a short period. Regularly check your credit report for errors and dispute any inaccuracies promptly.

6. Plan for Retirement

It's never too early to start saving for retirement. Contribute to employer-sponsored retirement plans like 401(k)s or individual retirement accounts (IRAs) to take advantage of tax benefits and employer matches. Consider your long-term financial needs and adjust your contributions over time to ensure you're on track for a comfortable retirement.

7. Invest for the Future

Investing can help grow your wealth over time and achieve financial goals such as buying a home, funding education, or building a nest egg. Educate yourself about different investment options, such as stocks, bonds, mutual funds, and real estate. Consider working with a financial advisor to develop an investment strategy based on your risk tolerance, time horizon, and financial objectives.

8. Build an Emergency Fund

An emergency fund provides a financial cushion to cover unexpected expenses like medical bills, car repairs, or job loss without resorting to borrowing money or dipping into savings earmarked for other goals. Aim to save three to six months' worth of living expenses in a liquid, accessible account.

9. Educate Yourself About Finances

Take the time to educate yourself about personal finance topics, including budgeting, investing, taxes, and insurance. Read books, attend workshops, or follow reputable financial websites and blogs for valuable insights and tips. The more you know about managing money, the better equipped you'll be to make informed financial decisions.

10. Seek Professional Guidance

If you're unsure about your financial situation or need assistance with complex financial matters, don't hesitate to seek guidance from a certified financial planner or advisor. They can provide personalized advice, help you set financial goals, and create a roadmap for achieving them.

Building healthy financial habits requires discipline, commitment, and ongoing effort. By creating a budget, saving regularly, managing debt wisely, and investing for the future, you can strengthen your financial foundation and achieve greater financial freedom. Start small, stay consistent, and celebrate your progress along the way. With time and dedication, you'll build the financial habits needed to secure a stable and prosperous future.

Chapter 15: Avoiding Common Debt Traps in the Future

Avoiding common debt traps is essential for maintaining financial health and avoiding unnecessary stress. Whether you've experienced debt problems in the past or want to prevent them altogether, understanding these pitfalls and adopting proactive strategies can help you stay on track towards financial stability.

1. Living Beyond Your Means

One of the most common debt traps is spending more than you earn. It's easy to fall into the temptation of buying things on credit or taking out loans to fund a lifestyle that isn't sustainable with your income. To avoid this trap:

- Create a Realistic Budget: Outline your income and expenses, including necessities and discretionary spending. Stick to your budget to ensure you live within your means.

- Avoid Impulse Purchases: Before making a purchase, ask yourself if it fits within your budget and if it's a necessity. Delaying non-essential purchases can help prevent unnecessary debt.

2. Relying Too Heavily on Credit Cards

Credit cards can be convenient but using them irresponsibly can lead to high-interest debt and financial strain. To avoid this trap:

- Use Credit Cards Wisely: Pay off your balance in full each month to avoid interest charges. If carrying a balance, prioritize paying more than the minimum to reduce interest costs.

- Monitor Your Spending: Keep track of credit card transactions to ensure you're not exceeding your budget. Set spending limits and stick to them.

3. Ignoring or Mismanaging Debt

Ignoring debt or mismanaging payments can quickly lead to financial trouble. To avoid this trap:

- Stay Organized: Keep track of all debts, payment due dates, and interest rates. Set up reminders or automatic payments to ensure bills are paid on time.
- Prioritize High-Interest Debt: Focus on paying off debts with the highest interest rates first while making minimum payments on others.

4. Not Having an Emergency Fund

Without an emergency fund, unexpected expenses can lead to reliance on credit cards or loans, increasing debt. To avoid this trap:

- Build an Emergency Fund: Save regularly to create a financial cushion for unexpected expenses. Aim to save three to six months' worth of living expenses in a separate, easily accessible account.

5. Overborrowing for Education or Housing

Student loans and mortgages can be substantial debts that impact your financial well-being for years. To avoid this trap:

- Research Affordable Options: Compare costs and consider community colleges or public universities for affordable education. Shop around for mortgages with favorable terms and reasonable interest rates.
- Borrow Responsibly: Only borrow what you need and can afford to repay. Avoid taking on excessive debt relative to your income.

6. Failing to Plan for Major Expenses

Large expenses like car repairs, medical bills, or home maintenance can strain finances if not planned for. To avoid this trap:

- Budget for Irregular Expenses: Set aside funds each month for future large expenses. Anticipate upcoming costs and plan accordingly to avoid relying on credit.

7. Neglecting Financial Education and Planning

Lack of financial knowledge and planning can lead to poor money management decisions and debt accumulation. To avoid this trap:

- Educate Yourself: Take advantage of resources such as personal finance books, workshops, or online courses to improve your financial literacy.

- Set Financial Goals: Establish short-term and long-term financial goals and create a plan to achieve them. Regularly review your progress and adjust as needed.

Avoiding common debt traps requires discipline, awareness, and proactive financial management. By living within your means, using credit responsibly, managing debt effectively, and planning for future expenses, you can build a solid financial foundation and avoid unnecessary debt stress. Start implementing these strategies today to safeguard your financial future and achieve lasting financial health.

Chapter 16: Resources and Tools for Debt Management

Managing debt effectively requires access to the right resources and tools to help you understand, organize, and pay off your debts. Whether you're looking for budgeting apps, debt calculators, or educational resources, here are some valuable tools and resources to support your debt management journey:

1. Budgeting Apps

Budgeting apps are convenient tools that can help you track income, expenses, and savings goals in real time. Some popular budgeting apps include:

- Mint: Tracks spending, creates budgets, and provides personalized financial insights.
- YNAB (You Need A Budget): Focuses on proactive budgeting and goal setting, helping users prioritize spending and save more.

- EveryDollar: Offers a zero-based budgeting approach, where every dollar has a designated purpose, helping users stay on track with their financial goals.

2. Debt Payoff Calculators

Debt payoff calculators help you visualize and plan for paying off your debts efficiently. These calculators typically allow you to input debt amounts, interest rates, and monthly payments to estimate the time and total cost of repayment. Examples include:

- Bankrate Debt Payoff Calculator: Calculates how long it will take to pay off debt based on different payment strategies.
- Credit Karma Debt Repayment Calculator: Estimates payoff timelines and interest savings based on additional payments.

3. Credit Counseling Agencies

Non-profit credit counseling agencies offer free or low-cost services to help consumers manage debt and improve financial literacy. They can provide personalized debt management plans, negotiate with creditors on your behalf, and offer financial education. Look for accredited agencies affiliated with the National Foundation for Credit Counseling (NFCC) or the Financial Counseling Association of America (FCAA).

4. Debt Consolidation Services

Debt consolidation services combine multiple debts into a single loan or payment plan with potentially lower interest rates. They can help simplify debt repayment and reduce monthly payments. Research reputable consolidation services and compare terms and fees before choosing a provider.

5. Financial Education Resources

Improving financial literacy is crucial for effective debt management. Explore these resources:

- Personal Finance Books: Books like "The Total Money Makeover" by Dave Ramsey or "Your Money or Your Life" by Vicki Robin provide practical advice on managing money and reducing debt.
- Online Courses: Platforms like Coursera, Udemy, or Khan Academy offer free or affordable courses on personal finance, budgeting, and debt management.
- Government Resources: Websites like USA.gov and the Consumer Financial Protection Bureau

(CFPB) offer guides and tools on managing debt, understanding credit, and consumer rights.

6. Debt Relief Programs

Debt relief programs, such as debt settlement or debt management plans (DMPs), can help negotiate with creditors to reduce the amount owed or establish manageable repayment terms. Be cautious and research reputable companies before enrolling in any debt relief program to avoid scams or high fees.

7. Credit Monitoring Services

Monitoring your credit is essential for detecting errors, identity theft, or unauthorized accounts. Services like Credit Karma, Experian, or Identity Guard provide free credit reports and monitoring services, alerting you to changes in your credit profile.

Utilizing these resources and tools can empower you to take control of your debt and improve your financial well-being. Whether you need assistance with budgeting, debt repayment strategies, or financial education, there are numerous options available to support you on your journey to becoming debt-free. Take advantage of these resources, educate yourself about personal finance, and develop a plan that aligns with your financial goals. With dedication and persistence, you can achieve financial stability and build a secure financial future.

Chapter 17: Real-life Success Stories

Real-life success stories of individuals overcoming debt and achieving financial freedom can inspire and provide valuable insights into effective debt management strategies. Here are a few captivating stories of people who turned their financial situations around:

1. Sarah's Journey to Debt Freedom

Sarah, a single mother of two, found herself drowning in credit card debt after unexpected medical expenses and job loss. Determined to regain control, she took proactive steps:

- Budgeting and Cutting Expenses: Sarah created a strict budget, cutting unnecessary expenses and focusing on essentials like groceries and utilities.

- Increasing Income: She took on a part-time job in the evenings and weekends to boost her income, using the extra earnings to pay down debt faster.

- Negotiating with Creditors: Sarah contacted her creditors to negotiate lower interest rates and payment plans that fit her budget.

Within three years, Sarah paid off over $30,000 in credit card debt. Today, she continues to prioritize saving and financial planning, teaching her children valuable money management skills.

2. Tom and Mary's Debt-Free Journey

Tom and Mary, a couple in their mid-30s, struggled with student loan debt and credit card balances for years. They decided to tackle their debt together:

- Debt Snowball Method: They used the debt snowball method, starting with their smallest debt and gradually paying off larger balances.

- Living Below Their Means: Tom and Mary made sacrifices, such as cooking at home more often and limiting discretionary spending, to free up more money for debt repayment.

- Seeking Professional Help: They enrolled in a debt management plan through a non-profit credit counseling agency, which helped negotiate lower interest rates and structured payments.

After five years of dedication and discipline, Tom and Mary became debt-free. They now focus on building savings, investing for the future, and enjoying financial security as a family.

3. John's Path to Financial Recovery

John, a recent college graduate, accumulated significant credit card debt while unemployed. Feeling overwhelmed, he sought guidance:

- Financial Education: John educated himself about personal finance through online resources and books, learning about budgeting, saving, and investing.

- Side Hustles: He started freelancing and tutoring to increase his income, using the extra money to pay off debt faster.

- Building an Emergency Fund: John prioritized building an emergency fund to cover unexpected expenses, preventing future reliance on credit cards. Within four years, John paid off his credit card debt and established healthy financial habits. He now mentors others on managing finances and avoiding debt traps.

These real-life success stories demonstrate that with determination, discipline, and effective strategies, it's possible to overcome debt and achieve financial freedom. Whether through budgeting, increasing income, negotiating with creditors, or seeking professional assistance, individuals can take control of their finances and build a secure future. By learning from these stories and applying proven debt management techniques, you too can embark on a journey towards financial stability and success.

Remember, every small step towards debt freedom brings you closer to your financial goals.

Chapter 18: Staying Debt-Free for Life

Achieving and maintaining a debt-free life is a rewarding accomplishment that provides financial security and peace of mind. Here are some key principles and strategies to help you stay debt-free for life:

1. Cultivate Healthy Financial Habits

Building and maintaining healthy financial habits is essential. This includes budgeting, saving regularly, living within your means, and avoiding unnecessary debt. Continuously monitor your spending and adjust your financial plan as needed to stay on track.

2. Build an Emergency Fund

An emergency fund acts as a financial buffer against unexpected expenses or income disruptions. Aim to save three to six months' worth of living expenses in a separate, easily accessible account. Having this fund in place can prevent the need to rely on credit during challenging times.

3. Avoid Impulse Purchases

Practice mindful spending by avoiding impulse purchases. Before making a purchase, consider whether it aligns with your financial goals and budget. Delaying non-essential purchases allows you to prioritize needs over wants and reduces the temptation to accumulate debt.

4. Pay Off Credit Card Balances Monthly

Credit cards can be convenient but carrying balances can lead to high-interest debt. Pay off credit card balances in full each month to avoid interest charges. If carrying a balance, prioritize paying more than the minimum to reduce interest costs and pay off debt faster.

5. Invest in Financial Education

Continuously educate yourself about personal finance topics such as budgeting, investing, and debt management. Stay informed about changes in financial markets and regulations that may impact your financial decisions. Knowledge empowers you to make informed choices and adapt to evolving financial circumstances.

6. Plan for Major Expenses

Anticipate large expenses such as home repairs, medical bills, or vehicle maintenance by budgeting and saving for them in advance. Planning ahead reduces the need to borrow money and helps maintain financial stability.

7. Monitor Your Credit Score

Regularly monitor your credit report to ensure accuracy and identify any potential issues early. A good credit score opens doors to favorable interest rates on loans and credit cards. Responsible credit management contributes to long-term financial health and stability.

8. Seek Professional Advice When Needed

If you encounter financial challenges or uncertainties, don't hesitate to seek advice from a certified financial planner or credit counselor. They can provide personalized guidance, help you create a financial plan, and offer strategies to achieve your financial goals.

Staying debt-free for life requires commitment, discipline, and proactive financial management. By adopting these principles and strategies, you can build a solid financial foundation, achieve financial freedom, and enjoy peace of mind knowing you're in control of your financial future. Remember, financial independence is a journey that rewards persistence and responsible decision-making. Start today and pave the way towards a debt-free and financially secure life.

Glossary of Financial Terms

Financial literacy is essential for making informed decisions about money management. This glossary provides definitions of key financial terms to enhance your understanding:

1. Budget: A financial plan that outlines expected income and expenses over a specific period, typically monthly or annually.

2. Credit Score: A numerical representation of an individual's creditworthiness based on credit history, ranging typically from 300 to 850.

3. Debt Consolidation: Combining multiple debts into a single loan or repayment plan to simplify payments and potentially lower interest rates.

4. Emergency Fund: Savings set aside to cover unexpected expenses or financial emergencies, reducing the need to rely on credit.

5. Interest Rate: The percentage charged by a lender for borrowing money, expressed annually as a percentage of the principal loan amount.

6. Asset: Any item of economic value owned by an individual or entity, which can be converted into cash.

7. Liability: Financial obligations or debts owed by an individual or entity, including loans, mortgages, and credit card balances.

8. Investment: Allocation of money into assets or securities such as stocks, bonds, mutual funds, or real estate with the expectation of generating income or profit.

9. Credit Card Utilization: The ratio of credit card balances to credit limits, influencing credit scores and financial health.

10. Compound Interest: Interest calculated on the initial principal and also on the accumulated interest of previous periods, leading to exponential growth of debt or savings over time.

11. Net Worth: The difference between an individual's assets and liabilities, indicating their overall financial position.

12. Foreclosure: Legal process by which a lender repossesses a property due to a borrower's failure to make mortgage payments.

13. IRA (Individual Retirement Account): A tax-advantaged retirement savings account that individuals can contribute to annually, with

contributions potentially deductible from taxable income.

14. 401(k): Employer-sponsored retirement savings plan where employees can contribute a portion of their salary, often with employer-matching contributions.

15. Compound Interest: Interest calculated on the initial principal and also on the accumulated interest of previous periods, leading to exponential growth of debt or savings over time.

16. Bankruptcy: Legal process for individuals or businesses unable to repay debts, providing relief from creditors while following court-approved repayment or liquidation plans.

17. Down Payment: Initial payment made when purchasing a home or other expensive asset, typically a percentage of the purchase price.

18. Credit Counseling: Professional advice and guidance provided by accredited agencies to help individuals manage debt, improve credit scores, and achieve financial goals.

19. Equity: Ownership interest in an asset after deducting any liabilities associated with it, representing the net value of the asset.

20. Amortization: Gradual repayment of a debt over time through scheduled installments, including both principal and interest.

www.ingramcontent.com/pod-product-compliance
Lightning Source LLC
Chambersburg PA
CBHW071931210526
45479CB00002B/632